PARCHMENT CRAFT

A fifteenth-century art form

*To my good friend and colleague
Carla Larter, who checked all the patterns,
and to Dolly, my mother, who fed,
watered and encouraged me.*

PARCHMENT CRAFT

A fifteenth-century art form

Janet Wilson

Search Press

First published in Great Britain 1995

Search Press Limited
Wellwood, North Farm Road,
Tunbridge Wells, Kent TN2 3DR

Reprinted 1996

ISBN 0 85532 796 0

There are references to sable brushes in this book. It is the
Publishers' custom to recommend synthetic materials as substitutes
for animal products wherever possible: many brushes made from
artificial fibres will be found to be as satisfactory as brushes made of
natural fibres.

Printed in Spain by A.G. Elkar S. Coop, 48012 Bilbao

Contents

Introduction   6

Materials and equipment   8

Tracing   11

Embossing with the 1.5mm tool   13

     Daisy birthday card   14
     Birthday card with numerals   18
     Floral-border card   20

Using the single-needle tool   22

     Floral fan   24
     Flower-garland card   26

Using the 3mm ball-tip tool   28

     Pansy bookmark   29
     Art-Nouveau fuchsias   31
     Valentine card   34

Embossing with the 1mm ball-tip and stylus tools   36

     Golden scrolls card   37
     Chrysanthemums and harebells   39

Colouring the paper with oil pastels   42

     Butterfly card   44
     Fantasy flowers and butterfly   48
     Christmas roses   51

Using the parchment scissors   54

     Flowers and trellis birthday card   55
     Religious card   57

Using the four-needle tool to make lace   59

     Lacy bookmark   62
     Carnival mask and orchid card   64
     Stylised butterfly   66

Cutting slots in lace work and freehand embossing   69

     Chinese New Year card   70
     Oval lace card   72
     Exotic bird   75

Cutting out large corners in lace work   77

     Victorian fuchsias   78

Index   80

Introduction

Parchment craft is an ancient art which is enjoying a tremendous revival in Europe and since 1991 in the United Kingdom when I first introduced the craft here. You do not have to be an artist to be able to do this craft; if you can hold a pen then you can have great fun with parchment craft.

Parchment craft is thought to have been used in Spanish cloisters in the fifteenth century, probably to decorate holy tracts or even bookbinding. Certainly, when you look at some of the early bookbinding done by Spanish and even French bookbinders, you will see that they have used parchment that has been washed in some compound to make it translucent and has then been embossed and pricked.

As the Church of Spain followed in the wake of Columbus to convert the natives of the New World, the Spaniards took with them not only their language and religion but also their ecclesiastical crafts. Today in South America parchment craft is still taught mostly in convent schools, and throughout South America various forms of this craft have evolved. The basic factor in all these different approaches to the same craft remains the same: embossing and perforating artificial parchment to produce raised patterns and lace-like designs. In Puerto Rico the general craft is actually called *tarjeteria pergaminada,* which basically means the art of creating greeting cards with parchment paper.

The tools originally used were very primitive: a needle tied to a piece of wood, an empty ballpoint pen or a knitting-needle, and a piece of felt for embossing. Today we are lucky in the fact that tools are now machine-made and that we have such things as the four-needle tool, which means we only have to mark the perforation once instead of four times with a single needle.

Parchment was originally made in the town of Pergamum in western Turkey as a substitute for papyrus. Parchment in its original form is the skin of sheep or goats, specially tanned for writing or painting on. Today, of course, we use a paper substitute.

There are variations of parchment craft in Mexico, Puerto Rico, Peru, Colombia and other countries in South America but the craft was brought back to Europe by a Colombian, Martha Ospina, who intro-duced the Colombian style of parchment craft to Holland and who taught me the craft. It was in Holland that I first saw this craft in 1990 and as a true paperholic I fell for it hook, line and embossing tool.

This book deals with the most important aspects of the craft – embossing and perforating. These are the foundations upon which the rest of the craft is built.

When you buy a pattern for a parchment-craft design, remember that you do not have to follow it to the letter: you can adapt it to suit yourself.

You can of course make up your own designs, which is great fun. Traditional parchment-craft motifs tend to be floral, but there is no reason why you cannot portray birds, animals, fruit, ribbons, musical motifs, heraldic designs, suns and moons . . . or add initials, names, banners or whatever you please.

If you like, you can also trace off the designs in the decorative oval panels at the beginning of the chapters, even though I have not shown the black and white patterns for them. Once you are hooked, you will find that you look for possible design ideas everywhere!

Materials and equipment

There are a number of products made especially for this craft,
and these or similar items can be bought in many craft shops or
via mail-order specialists (see page 80).

Paper

The most important thing is the correct type of paper.
While the craft is called parchment craft, in fact the
paper we use is pseudo-parchment; it weighs 150
grammes per square metre. This paper is specially treated
to stop it cracking when folded and to facilitate easier
embossing. You can buy it in A5, A4 and A3 size packs
(approximately 8¼ x 5⅞in, 11¾ x 8¼in and 16½ x
11¾in).

Pad

You will need a pad for embossing on and later on a felt-
type pad for use when you are perforating. You can use
the felt pad for embossing as well but it is a little soft.
You will find that you get the best results by using the
embossing pads that are sold for the purpose.

Embossing tools

There are a number of embossing tools you can buy. I
have referred to them throughout this book by their
size. To find out the size of your tool, lay the ball end on
a metric ruler with the widest part of the ball against a
millimetre marking and then read off how wide it is.

Needle tools

There are specially made one-, two- and four-needle
tools on the market, as well as some fancy-shaped
needle tools from South America which are used for
more advanced work. There is even a three-needle tool

*A good range of materials for parchment craft
– but of course you can start this craft with
just a small selection of equipment.*

with the needles laid out in a triangular format, which can be used in more advanced lace work.

Scissors

These need to have short curved blades and fine points. There are some that are made especially for parchment craft.

You can also use deckle-edged or pinking scissors to cut the outside edges of straight-edged cards, or you can use these on the inserts when you trim them to size after sewing them into the card.

Pen

A school-type mapping pen is used for tracing designs with inks.

Ink

Use waterproof ink in white, gold and silver: there are many available, including one made especially for this craft. Remember to replace the top on the bottle as soon as you have finished tracing or the ink will thicken.

Oil pastels

You will need a set of oil pastels for colouring your designs. There are many varieties to choose from, but you should take care to buy one that does not crumble when applied to the paper. You will also need some medium for spreading the oil pastels, such as white spirit or barbecue igniter; this is discussed in the chapter on the use of oil pastels (see page 43).

Inserts

Inserts can be made from virtually any type of coloured paper and you can also buy commercially printed white inserts with a variety of greetings from companies who specialise in supplying blank cards, etc., to craftspeople. For sewing in inserts you will need a needle and some metallic thread or coloured fine crochet cotton, depending on the colour coordination you want.

Envelopes

Envelopes for your cards can be obtained at any good office stationery shop at a reasonable price, or you can obtain these through one of the companies who specialise in blank cards and envelopes for craftspeople. You can even make your own envelopes from coloured paper.

Sending the cards through the post should be no problem but I do recommend that you put in a piece of card to stiffen the envelope.

Paintbrush

You will need a fine sable-hair paintbrush: either No. 1 or No. 2. If you do not use a real hair brush you will find that you will have problems keeping the brush end pointed. The sable-hair brush will keep its pointed end, while the synthetic-hair one will splay out, causing you problems. Never leave your brush or mapping pen in water – you will spoil the brush and rust the pen.

Sometimes embossing tools can seem to snag on the paper. If this happens, you can grease the tool by rubbing it on the greasy spot on your chin, or on your hair, or by dipping it in a small pot of beeswax such as lace-makers use. Alternatively, there is a special product on the market for this craft.

Other materials

The other things you will require include a white pencil for marking the fold lines (and, in some cases, the card edges), a ruler, kitchen paper, and a small container for water.

Tracing

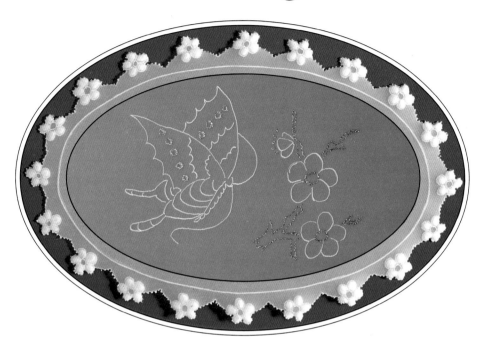

All the designs are traced on to the parchment with a mapping pen. The best pen to use is a cheap 'school-type' mapping pen and holder. The graphic mapping pens whip too much, as the length between the nib point and the reservoir is too long. The fine tracing line that you are aiming for is produced not by the size of the nib but by the manner in which you hold the pen. Remember to dip a new nib into boiling water to improve its writing qualities, or suck it – but do be careful!

Secure the parchment paper to the pattern by using two small pieces of sticky tape rolled into a cylinder sticky side out. Place a piece at opposite corners, avoiding the pattern area. This will ensure that the paper does not slip when you are tracing and you can also leave it if you are called away and then come back and safely finish the tracing of the pattern.

White ink needs shaking before use. Also, as it is waterproof when dry and therefore will not wash out, make sure that you place it in a position where you will not knock it over while working. If you do have an accident and spill ink on yourself or on to the working area, quickly mop it up with kitchen paper before it dries. Use a dampened piece of kitchen paper to remove ink from clothes.

Wash your nib in water and dry it with a piece of kitchen paper before dipping into the ink. Do this every time you need more ink – wash, dry and dip. If you prefer, you can use a small sponge soaked in water and placed on a small dish: wipe your nib on this (no need to dry) and then dip again. Only dry the nib when you are putting the pen away or changing colour.

Try out your tracing techniques on a spare piece of paper so that you do not spoil your first complete piece. There is often a spare piece above or to one side of the pattern which, as it will be cut away, can be used for trying out the pen on. If you hold the pen in the upright position and let it glide across the paper you will draw a very fine line, which is what we are aiming for. If you press down on the pen, the nib splays and makes a thick line, which will look ugly on your finished design. Remember that practice makes perfect – you will soon get the hang of holding the pen in the upright position and letting it glide across the paper.

If you have a 'wobbly' hand, some people have found it helps to rest their hand on the felt pad while tracing. If you go over a line this will not matter, as you are taking away the pattern when you have finished, so no one will know that you have missed the line!

Tracing with gold and silver inks

The technique for tracing with gold or silver inks is slightly different, and the pen is held in the pencil position so that a thicker line is produced. Again, the bottle of ink must be shaken well to ensure that the suspension mixes with the gold powder or silver paste. If you dip into these metallic inks with your nib all you are likely to get is suspension, so the nib is filled in a different manner. Use a plastic stirrer (the type used in fast-food outlets for stirring coffee) or a spatula and stir up the ink, making sure that you get right to the bottom of the bottle, then drip the ink from the stirrer into the ink reservoir of your pen. When you want to fill in a wide gold or silver border, trace the edges with the pen and then, once more using the plastic stirrer, fill your paintbrush with gold ink and paint in between the gold lines. Again, you must wash and dry your pen or brush between filling them. Remember that gold/silver ink takes longer to dry than the non-metallic inks, so be careful not to smudge your design.

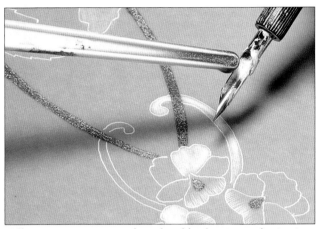

Filling a mapping-pen nib with gold ink using a plastic stirrer.

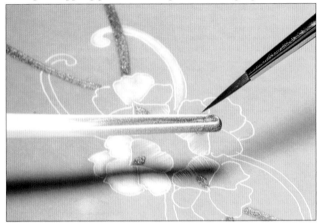

Filling a paintbrush with gold ink using a plastic stirrer.

Tracing a straight line

Use a ruler bevel side down to the paper and draw along this. Always make sure that you have enough ink on the pen and also wipe the ruler between lines. If you only have a straight-sided ruler (with no bevel side), then attach a small, thin coin to either end of the ruler with sticky tape and this will raise the edge off the paper.

Tips to help you trace better

Always try the pen on a spare piece of paper before tracing, as sometimes the pen does not seem to want to work, particularly with metallic inks.

If you have a problem with ink flow, hold the pen upright on a spare piece of paper for a few moments and then try it again. If it still does not want to work after several attempts at this, wash it, dry it and fill it again.

An old pen nib works best with metallic inks – so treat yourself to two pens and keep the newest nib for non-metallic inks and the oldest for metallic inks.

To protect the paper from getting marked by your hand while working, use a piece of kitchen paper under your hand.

Embossing with the 1.5mm tool

Embossing is done from the back of the paper, so after tracing your design, turn your paper over and place it on to the soft side of the embossing pad. The 1.5mm ball-tip tool is the most used of all the embossing tools and is the tool that a beginner should start embossing with.

To emboss, rub the tool in your chosen area; for instance, a flower petal. Rub gently to start with, going from side to side and keeping within the traced outline of the petal. Each time you rub, exert a little more pressure and you will see the paper start to change colour as you displace the fibres in the paper.

After a few passes over the area you will feel the paper become more elastic and then you can rub harder. If the shape is round, you can start to go round and round with the tool and you will end up with a snow-white raised design on the right side of the paper.

If you go round and round to start with you will get a small black mark in the middle of your petal which is virtually impossible to get rid of. Check your progress as you go along: if the petal still looks grey, rub harder, as you should end up with a white, raised design.

It is now time to start practising tracing and use of the 1.5mm embossing tool with the first pattern – the daisy birthday card.

This card uses a sheet of A5 (8¼ x 5⅞in) parchment paper or half a sheet of A4 (11¾ x 8¼in). The roughest side of the paper is the side that you trace on. If you remember to say to yourself 'rough is right', you will always have the paper the best way round.

Daisy birthday card

Full-size pattern.

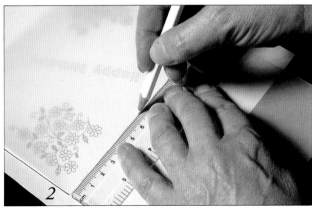

1. Using a small piece of cellulose tape, fasten the A5 (8¼ x 5⅞in) piece of parchment paper to the pattern as explained on page 11, remembering that you will only be tracing on one half as the other half is the back of the card when folded.

2. Mark the fold line with a ruler and a white pencil using a dashed line.

3. Trace the pattern of flowers and leaves and the greeting with white ink, remembering to keep the pen in the upright position so that the tracing lines are as fine as possible.

When you have finished tracing the design, carefully remove the parchment paper from the pattern.

4. Turn the paper over and place it on the soft side of an embossing pad. Carefully emboss the greeting; you will find it easier to follow the line of the letter – that is, the two uprights of the letter H and then the crossbar.

On some patterns available from craft shops to give you guidance as to what is to be embossed, some of the areas have been marked in black. This indicates areas to be embossed and also means that you must emboss the same shapes on other parts of the same pattern.

5. Now emboss the flowers. As the petals of the flowers are more elongated, rub the tool up and down the petal until you feel the paper starting to stretch, then go up round the petal outline, not over it, and finish off embossing so that when you turn the paper over, your flower petal is really white. Emboss each petal the same way, but do not emboss the centres of the flowers.

Sewing in inserts

To finish the card off, choose a piece of coloured notepaper, typing paper or art paper and fold it in half. Fold the card in half also and then, using metallic thread and a needle, stitch the coloured insert into the card as described below. Use this method of putting inserts into all your cards. You can also at the same time stitch in a commercially printed greeting insert. Once the insert is stitched into place, you can trim it to match the outside edge of the card, using sharp scissors, a craft knife or a sliding roller cutter (the modern-day successor to the guillotine, with a sharp sliding blade).

1. First, fold the inserts. Then, putting the insert or inserts into the card, use the single-needle tool to prick three or five holes, depending on how large your card is, through all the layers.

2. If you are sewing a three-hole insert, start in the middle hole, going from inside to out, up to the top hole, then straight down to the bottom hole and so back to the middle hole from outside to in. Then you can knot it and tie a bow. If you want your bow on the outside of the card, reverse the first instruction.

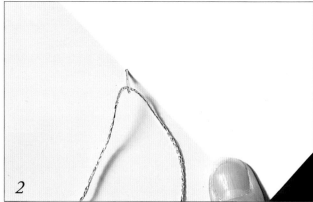

3. Carry on like this down through all the other holes and you should finish with the thread on the inside. This can then be knotted and tied in a bow.

For five holes, start sewing with the middle hole from inside to out, then up to the next hole. The needle goes from outside to inside, up to the next hole from inside to outside, then back down to the next hole down, which you will have used once already.

The finished card.

Birthday card with numerals

Here you have a choice of birthday numbers. Just trace the whole of the design and then fit in the number of your choice in the centre of the wreath.

Fold line

Happy

40
th

Birthday

1234567890 th st nd

Full-size pattern.

The finished card.

Tracing

Mark the fold line with a ruler and white pencil and also use white pencil to draw the scalloped edge of the card. Using white ink, trace the greeting, the wreath of flowers, and the numerals of your choice.

Embossing

Emboss the double outlines of the greeting and age and then the the flower petals – not the centres.

Finishing off

Fold the card in half and stitch in the insert of your choice. Using sharp scissors, cut round the edge of the card following the marked lines. (You could also perforate the card out using the single-needle tool: see page 22 to find out how to do this).

Floral-border card

This pattern also uses a sheet of A5 (8¼ x 5⅞in) paper.

Fold line

Full-size pattern.

Tracing

With the white pencil, mark the fold line, and with white ink trace the whole of the design.

Embossing

Using the 1.5mm tool, emboss the flowers in the border design and the flowers in the central design but not the centres. Then emboss the two buds but not the leaves under them.

Perforating

With the needle tool, pierce the centres of the flowers in the border, using the felt pad under the card and not the embossing pad.

Finishing off

Fold the card and sew in the insert of your choice.

The finished card.

Using the single-needle tool

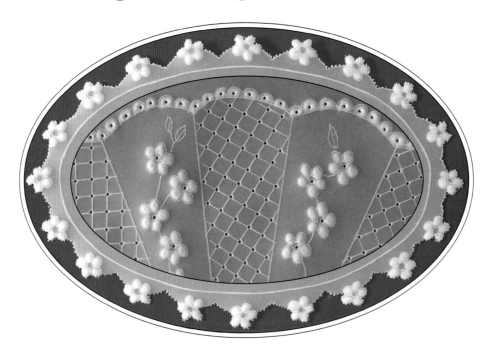

Perforating round an edge

The distinctive edges on parchment-craft cards are created by perforating with either a single-needle or a two-needle tool. Place the folded card complete with its sewn-in insert on to the felt pad and with the single-needle tool held in the *upright* position push the needle through all four layers of the card, making sure that the needle is pushed right down as far as it will go each time.

The holes should be very close together so that when you have finished the waste paper can be easily removed. This is easier to do with the two-needle tool, but you do have to be careful to make sure that *both* needles are on the outline you are following.

The most common mistake people make when they start perforation work is that they do not let the needle tool travel the full needle length through the paper. If you only use the tip of the tool then the holes will not be large enough and the paper will not tear away.

Another common fault is making the holes too far apart. They need to be close together to achieve the right effect and to allow easy removal of the waste

paper. If you have a two-needle tool then you will see that the needles are only one millimetre apart: this is the correct distance you should allow between the holes. If you are using a single-needle tool you will find that judging the distance will come with practice.

Perforating round an edge is not achieved in a few seconds. It takes time, particularly if it is the first time you have tried it. Please have patience – the finished result is well worth it and with practice you will get much quicker. Remember that if you are impatient you could very well tear your whole design when you come to remove the waste paper.

To remove the waste paper, press down on the waste edge close to the perforation line. Use the soft side of the embossing pad to lay your card on to do this, and if you have perforated correctly the paper will start to give way on the perforation line. If it does not do so immediately, try another part of the perforation. Once the perforations have started to tear away cleanly, you can gently ease the rest of it away.

Perforating. Note the way the tool is held for this operation.

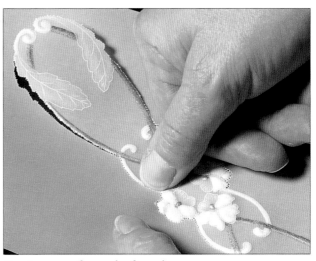

Pressing out a fancy edge from the waste paper.

Tip: I usually remove the waste parchment paper from both sides once I have got the perforations to start tearing away cleanly and then I remove the insert paper waste, rather than trying to remove all four layers at once. It is usually easier to press down at the fold edge when trying to start the perforations breaking away.

Using the single-needle tool as an embossing tool

The single-needle tool need not only be used for perforating; it also makes a super-fine embossing tool. There are occasions when you want to emboss a very fine line in a small flower petal, for instance, and this tool is ideal for this and also for making the fine vein lines in leaves.

So from now on, instead of tracing in the veins of leaves, why not try embossing them in freehand with the single-needle tool, using the pattern for guidance. You will see that the effect is much more delicate.

The single-needle tool is also wonderful when you want to draw cross-hatching or grid lines on your card. Again, instead of tracing them, use the single-needle tool to draw them in – the effect is so much better. The two-needle tool can also be used for drawing lines that you want to be of equal distance from each other.

To use the single needle as an embossing tool, hold it in the pencil position as you would any other type of embossing tool. It needs to be in the upright position, of course, when you are using it for perforating work.

Embossing with the single-needle tool.

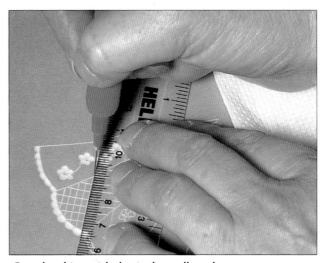

Cross-hatching with the single-needle tool.

Floral fan

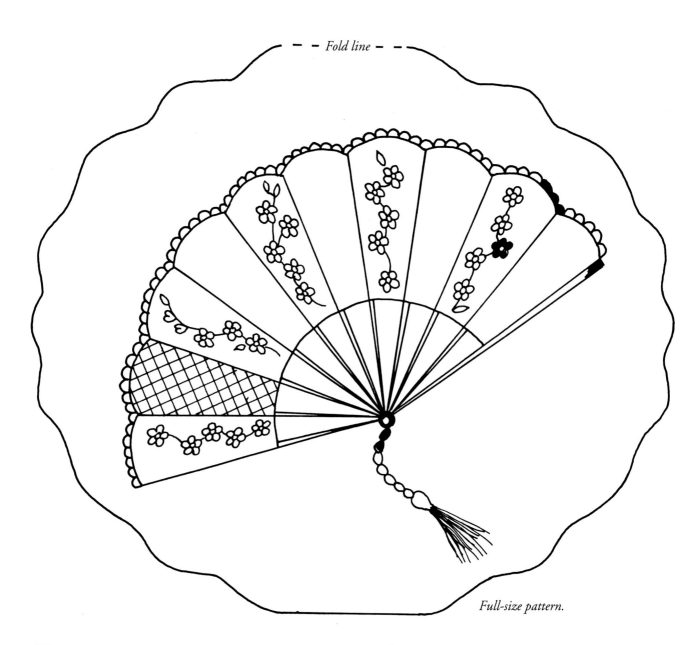

- - Fold line - - -

Full-size pattern.

Tracing

With white pencil, mark out the fold line and the shaped edge of the card.

Using white ink, trace the fan but do not trace the cross-hatching shown on one of the fan segments, nor the end of the tassel.

Embossing

With the 1.5mm tool, emboss the flower petals, the scalloped top edge, the fan sticks and the ring hinge. Emboss the tassel cord by going round the outer edge of the pattern, leaving the middle of each piece of cord free of embossing (see the picture of the card) and then

The finished card.

emboss the head of the tassel fully. With the single-needle tool and a ruler, draw in the cross-hatching in each of the remaining empty sections. Draw in the tassel ends freehand with the single-needle tool.

Tip: If you are using a transparent ruler you can use the markings as a guide to enable you to keep the cross-hatched lines at the same distance from each other. Draw the first line with the tool and then move the ruler up so that the chosen marking rests against the first line, and so on.

Perforating

Pierce a hole in the middle of each embossed scallop on the top edge of the fan, in the middle of each flower, and in the middle of the ring hinge. Also pierce a hole where the lines in the cross-hatching intersect.

Finishing off

Fold the card in half and sew in the insert, then perforate round the shaped edge with the single-needle tool or the two-needle tool, going through all four layers, and then remove waste parchment and insert paper.

Flower-garland card

Fold line

Best Wishes

Full-size pattern.

Tracing

Mark the fold line and the edges of the card with white pencil and trace the flowers and greetings in white ink.

Embossing

With the 1.5mm ball-tip tool, emboss the flower centres as well as the leaves and stalks that appear under every

other flower. Emboss the greeting. With the single-needle tool, emboss fine lines on the flowers without stalks, working from the outside edge towards the centre and making sure that the lines are close together. Again using the single-needle tool, emboss the other flowers from the centre towards the outer edge.

Finishing off

Fold the card and sew in the insert of your choice and then trim the card edges with sharp scissors or fancy-edged scissors to taste.

The finished card.

Using the 3mm ball-tip tool

As an artist uses different brushes to obtain different effects, so we use different sizes of embossing tools to create different shades and effects. The larger the tip of the embossing tool the greyer the effect, and the smaller the tip of the tool the whiter the effect will be.

This large ball-tipped tool makes it easier to emboss in large areas, particularly when embossing in a double-outline border. The best way I have found to emboss a double-outline border is to use the 3mm ball-tip tool and emboss all the way along one side from corner to corner at one pressure, then go along again at a slightly heavier pressure. Continue in this way until you are satisfied with the embossing and then start the next corner-to-corner piece. If you use this technique you will avoid getting lumps and bumps in borders which detract from the finished work. Once you have made

Embossing a double outline with the 3mm tool.

Embossing a large area with the wrong end of the tool.

several passes over the border area you can then use the 1.5mm ball tip to finish off with, again using the same technique, and this will produce a whiter finish.

For a very large area, or where you want to colour the paper only slightly, reverse the embossing tool and use the plastic end. In a large area I very often start with the reverse end of the tool and then finish off with the metal end.

Pansy bookmark

Tracing

With gold ink (see the chapter on *Tracing*), trace the two curved arms going up and down from the flower centre but *not* the two small leaves at the bottom or the two large leaves and their scrolls at the top. Also trace in gold the tiny teardrop centres in the flowers. Trace the rest of the design in white ink but *not* the veins in the leaves.

Painting

With gold ink (see the chapter on *Tracing* for how to fill the brush with ink), fill in the double gold outline of arms – see the picture of the finished article for guidance.

Embossing

With the 3mm ball tip, emboss the gold arms at both ends of the bookmark and also the four other arms which extend from the flower centre. Emboss the top four leaves of each pansy with the 3mm tool. Using the reverse end of the tool emboss the leaves at each end of the bookmark, and then, reversing the tool, emboss the scroll ends of the top leaves up to where the main leaf starts. With the single-needle tool, emboss fine lines on the bottom petal of each pansy, starting from the lower line and working towards the centre (the lines should not reach further than approximately half way up the petal). Also with the single-needle tool, draw in the veins on the four leaves and draw three lines on each fully embossed petal of the pansy, working from the

Full-size pattern.

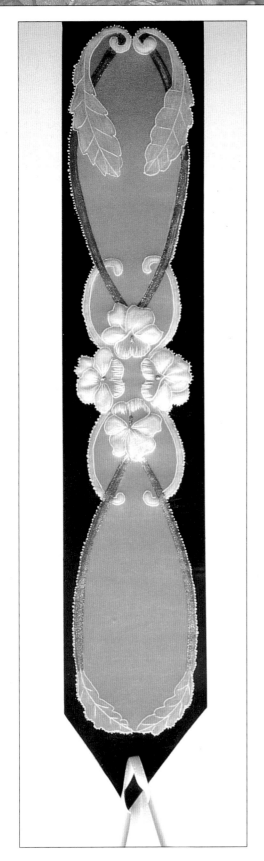

middle towards the outer edge. With the 1.5mm tool, emboss the centres of the flowers.

Perforating

With the single- or two-needle tool, perforate round the outside edge of the bookmark and remove the waste paper.

Finishing off

The perforated bookmark will fit into a commercial bought bookmark sleeve 4cm (1½in) wide. Push the bookmark in carefully until it touches the sealed top and trim the bottom to about 1.5cm (½in) below the bottom of the bookmark. Punch a hole in the centre of the bottom and thread through a short length of 1.5–3mm (¹/₁₆–¹/₈in) wide ribbon. See the picture of the finished bookmark for guidance.

Variations

As with many of the parchment-craft patterns in this book, you can vary the design. In this case the bookmark will look entirely different if you just trace it in white ink instead of using gold and white ink as we have done in this example.

The finished bookmark.

Art-Nouveau fuchsias

Detail of the photograph on page 33.

Tracing

In gold, ink the scrolls of the border but not the two bottom corner flowers. Also do the leaf above the flowers, the veining, the two scrolls and the pointed line underneath the flowers. The rest of the design is traced in white ink.

Painting

Using gold ink and a paintbrush, fill in the scroll that extends from the middle of the corner flowers in the border and the two scrolls and pointed line beneath the flower design.

Embossing

With the 3mm tool, emboss the areas between the double-outlined border scrolls, the top middle section of each flower, the two upward-curling petals on each side of the flowers, the two petals at the bottom of the flower at each side of the middle petal, and the two scrolls that extend downwards from the flower design. With the reverse end of the tool, emboss the gold outlined leaf at the top. With the 1.5mm tool, emboss the curled-up section only of the two petals at each side of the main petal, the pointed line that extends from the bottom of the flower design and the two gold scrolls that extend from the corner border flowers.

With the single-needle tool, emboss the petals of the two corner flowers, starting at the outside edge and working toward the centre. Then emboss the bottom edge of the main petal in each flower, the section of petal behind the curled-up edge on the two petals either side of the main petal, working from the embossed area toward the main petal, and the very tips of the two outermost petals that extend from the two upward-curling petals on each flower. Also with the single-needle tool, draw a line extending from just below the round top of each main petal to the middle bottom of the main petal (see photograph of finished card for guidance).

Finishing off

Fold the card in half and sew in any inserts.

Fold line

Full-size pattern.

The finished card.

Valentine card

Fold line

Full-size pattern.

Tracing

Mark the fold line and card edge with white pencil. Gold-ink the greeting, then do the rest of the design in white ink except the veining in the leaves and the stalks of the tiny ball-like flowers.

Painting

With gold ink and a paintbrush, fill in the double-outlined letter in the greeting.

Embossing

With the 3mm tool, emboss the double-outline border. With the reverse end of the tool, emboss the leaves and the petals of the flower. With the 1.5mm tool, emboss the ball-like flowers and the anthers in the middle of the flower, as well as the gold-painted letter in the greeting. With the single needle, draw in the leaf veins and the stalks of the ball-like flowers, using the pattern as a guide. Also emboss fine lines on each petal, working from the outside edge towards the centre (see the picture of the finished card for guidance) and finally draw in the stamens with the needle tool.

Perforating and finishing off

Fold the card and stitch in a scarlet insert.

Using either the single-needle or the two-needle tool, perforate round the edge of the card, going through all the layers and using the white pencil line as a guide. Start at one side of the fold line and work round to the other side of the fold line.

The finished card.

Embossing with the 1mm ball-tip and stylus tools

The 1mm ball-tip tool is best used in very small areas; it gives an ultra-white embossing. Use the tool in exactly the same way as you would use the 1.5mm ball tip; that is, start from side to side or up and down a petal or small circle before going round and round with the tool. If you use this technique you will find that you end up with a more even embossing and you do not end up with a tiny black hole in the centre of small circle-like embossings.

This tool is often used in conjunction with the stylus tool when embossing freehand petals in lace grids.

The stylus-type tool is used in a similar manner to that you use when you are using the single-needle tool as an embossing tool. This tool produces thicker lines and is best used in large flower petals and leaves. You can also use this tool to freehand in any lines to which you would like to give a raised effect.

A word of warning: it is well-nigh impossible to follow a traced line with the stylus tool. You usually end up with a thick, ugly double line somewhere along the line you are following. So if you want a line border within your card edge, use the tool with a ruler and draw in the border freehand.

If the line you want to emboss is a curved line, draw the line with the white pencil and then use the stylus tool, as you can rub out any white pencil line that you have not managed to follow.

Golden scrolls card

Fold line

Full-size pattern.

Tracing

With gold, ink the single-line border and the three scrolls extending from the central flowers. Trace the double-line outer edge of the card and the flowers and leaves with white ink.

Painting

With gold ink, fill in the double scroll outlines traced in gold.

Embossing

With the 3mm tool, followed by the 1.5mm tool, emboss the area within the double outline around the edge of the card. With the 3mm tool, gently emboss the leaves to a pale grey colour and also emboss the golden scrolls.

Using the 1.5mm tool, emboss the centres of the two flowers. With the 1mm tool, emboss the tiny circles surrounding the twigs. Using the stylus tool, draw lines close together extending from the outer edge of each petal towards the centre of the flowers. With the single-needle tool, draw in the vein lines on each leaf freehand.

Finishing off

Fold the card in half and sew in any insert as required. Cut the card edges on a roller cutter or with sharp scissors round the outer edge of the embossed border line, using the outer white line as a guide.

The finished card.

Chrysanthemums and harebells

Tracing

Mark the fold line with a white pencil and also the outer edges of the card.

With gold ink, trace the outlines of the double border. The main design of flowers is traced in white ink.

Painting

If you like, fill in the double gold border edges with gold ink.

Embossing

With the 3mm tool, emboss the harebells and buds to a pale grey – do *not* emboss the harebell that is showing the bottom of the bell only. Emboss the area within the double-border line. Also gently emboss the leaves of the chrysanthemums, the two large leaves and the double-outline stalks. Using the 1mm ball tip, emboss the upper leaves of each harebell and bud where they join the stems; also emboss the stamens denoted by the tiny round circles. With the 1.5mm ball tip, emboss the upward-curling petals of the top chrysanthemum; on the lower chrysanthemum emboss the two narrow petals at the bottom and the narrow upward-curling one.

Emboss the double-outline stalks, again using the 1.5mm tool, and also the edges of the large leaves (see the photograph of the finished card for guidance).

With the stylus, emboss fine lines on each chrysanthemum petal, working from the bottom of the petal towards the centre.

From the right side of the paper, using the stylus tool, emboss a fine line on the fluted edges of the harebells, working from the bottom edge upwards. With the 1.5mm tool, emboss the lower petals of the top chrysanthemum – the ones that look as though they are behind the stalk – and also the two diamond shapes which depict the back of the bottom two harebell fluted edges.

From the back, using the single-needle tool draw in the stamens, working from the anthers toward the flower, and draw in the leaf veins on the two large and the two small leaves.

Finishing off

Fold the card on the fold line and sew in any insert as required. Cut round the edges of the card.

Embossing using the same tools but choosing different flowers.

Fold line

Full-size pattern.

The finished card.

Colouring the paper with oil pastels

You can change the colour of the parchment paper by applying oil pastels to the back of the paper. The colour can be applied to the whole page or to the front page of a card, and can be applied in stripes or in specific areas. The pastels can also be mixed on the paper.

It is best to work on a plasticised surface when applying oil pastels, so that any pastel that comes over the edge of the paper can be wiped from the work surface.

Some of the dark colours can stain a surface, so it is better to find or make yourself a board that is kept only for this type of work.

To make one of these boards for yourself, use a piece of A3 (16½ x 11¾in) thick card and cover it with self-adhesive clear plastic (the sort that is used to protect book covers, etc.). Otherwise, just work on scrap card which you can discard after the colouring process.

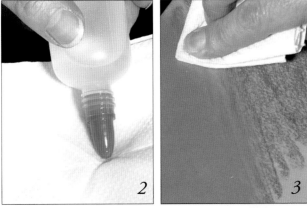

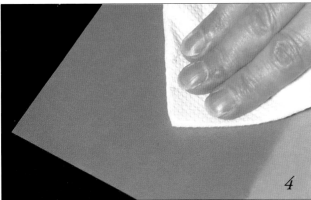

Colouring a complete sheet of parchment paper

1. Turn the paper over so that the smoother side is uppermost, and, using the flat surface of the oil pastel (some have pointed ends), rub the pastel evenly over the paper, working diagonally.

2. Fold a piece of kitchen paper into four and put a couple of drops of medium in the middle. Everyone seems to have their own favourite medium. I prefer to use colourless barbecue igniter, which is virtually odour-free, but some people use white spirit or other art mediums. Whichever medium you choose, please work in an airy room and do not smoke.

3. The next job is to even out the colour and remove the excess pastel. Paler colours can usually be evened out by rubbing the surface with a folded piece of kitchen paper, which will remove the excess pastel and give you an even, pale colour. The darker colours need some medium to spread them. Fold the paper into four again and start wiping it over the paper in the same direction as you applied the pastel. If you have too much medium on the paper you will find that it will wipe the paper clean; too little and it will not spread the pastel evenly.

4. When you have finished, wipe the area of the card with a clean piece of folded kitchen paper. This will remove any excess medium and pastel from the parchment. Also wipe the edges of the parchment paper clean. You should end up with a delicately, evenly coloured piece of paper.

5. Finally, take the paper you have coloured, turn it over, and carefully affix it to the pattern. Be careful where you place the sticky tape as this will remove the colour from your paper.

Then trace the design, remove the paper from the pattern, turn it over, and emboss it in the normal way from the back (you can see the effect of this in the picture of the butterfly on the next page).

The embossing will show up white on the right side and the overall effect of white tracing and embossing on a coloured background gives a totally different slant to any of the patterns that we have already covered in this book.

Try the technique out on the pattern for the butterfly card over the page.

Butterfly card

Tracing

Mark the fold line with white pencil. Trace the whole of the design, including the edges, in white.

Oil pastels

Colour the area of the front page with coloured pastel of your choice and smooth out with medium.

Embossing

Emboss the flowers in the border with the 1.5mm tool. Emboss the double inner border and the body of the butterfly with the 3mm tool.

With the single-needle tool, cross-hatch the circles in the butterfly's wings and emboss the rest of the design in the wings with the 1.5mm tool, including the ends of the antennae. Emboss the greeting. With the stylus tool, emboss stripes on the butterfly's body and also stalks on the flowers in the border area (see the photograph for guidance).

Finishing off

With the single-needle tool, perforate those of the flower petals that overlap the fold line and then fold the card. The flower petals should now stand out from the fold line. Sew in any insert and then, using the single-needle tool, perforate round the petals that protrude from the edge of the card. Finally, using either the single- or the two-needle tool, perforate the scallops on the white traced line so that this disappears on the finished card.

Reverse side of the butterfly card, showing the parchment paper coloured with oil pastel.

Fold line

Best Wishes

Full-size pattern.

The finished card.

Rainbow colouring with oil pastels

This method gives a graded coloured background, so choose colours that blend together well. I am particularly fond of magenta, dark blue and violet. An autumnal combination can be made with brown, yellow and orange; or try green, yellow and brown. Even two different shades of the same colour can look good. Remember that the oil pastel will not be as dark as it appears in the stick once you have spread it on the parchment paper.

I usually work on the diagonal for the best striped effect, but you can work in box-like squares, starting with a solid middle and adding a border of another colour, followed by a border of a third colour. You could even make it circular, starting with one colour and adding bands of different colours. Whichever you choose, the method is the same.

Start with your first chosen colour and make a band at least 2.5cm (1in) wide. Apply it using the flat end of the pastel; then, leaving a tiny gap, apply a band of the next colour, remembering to make it at least 2.5cm (1in) wide. Next, leaving a tiny gap, apply a band of the third colour. Repeat this process, starting with the first colour again, until you have covered the area you wish to be coloured.

Using your chosen medium on a piece of kitchen paper, spread the bands of the same colour. Change the kitchen paper round to get a clean bit and spread the bands of the second colour. Finally, again changing the kitchen paper round, spread the bands of the third colour. If you do not turn the kitchen paper so that you have a clean piece for each colour, you will transfer one colour on to the next.

Then, again choosing a clean area of the kitchen paper, work the area between the stripes so that they blend one into the other. Here, again, I usually work the stripes of the same colour at one time and then change the kitchen paper round and blend the next sets of areas between the stripes. Once you have finished blending, use a clean piece of dry kitchen paper and rub off any excess medium and colour. Make sure you have a clean area for each stripe and the area where they blend one into the other. You should end up with a delicately coloured rainbow effect.

Try this out on the pattern on page 48.

Applying the oil pastel.   *Spreading the colour.*

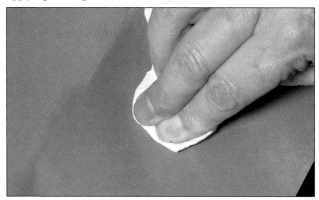
Blending the edges of the stripes.

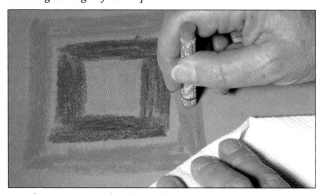
An alternative way of applying the colour – in squares.

Softening the edges of the squares for a misty effect.

Fantasy flowers and butterfly

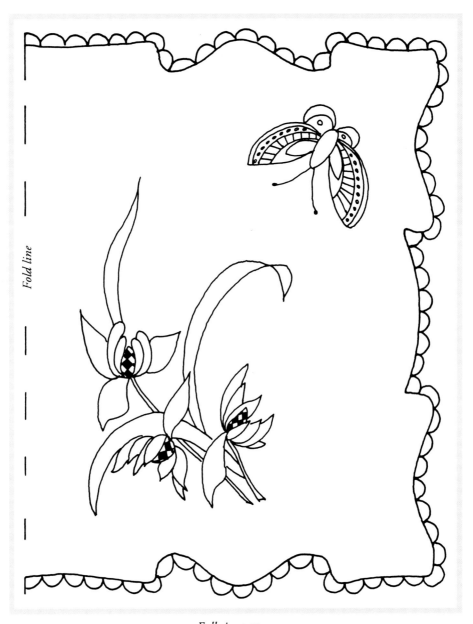

Fold line

Full-size pattern.

Tracing

Mark the fold line with white pencil and ruler. With gold ink, trace the dots on the butterfly wings and the two inner eye-shaped areas on the top set of wings, then the two petals on each side of the chequerboard centre of each flower. With white ink, trace the rest of the design (not the butterfly feelers) and the border.

Oil pastels

Colour the front page only. Using three colours of your choice, start in the top right-hand corner and put on bands of colour each at least 2.5cm (1in) wide. When you have applied a band of each colour, start again with the first colour and apply bands until the area is covered – approximately five bands of colour in all. Then spread

the colours and blend the area between the stripes so that one colour blends into the next. Finish off by wiping each area with a clean, dry piece of kitchen paper.

Painting

Using gold ink, fill in the traced outline of the eye shape in the upper pair of butterfly wings and the two petals on either side of the chequerboard centre of each flower.

Embossing

Emboss the semi-circular shapes round the border edge, using the 3mm tool to 'warm' the paper up, and then follow this with the 1.5mm tool to give a really white appearance. Next, emboss between the double outer lines of each butterfly wing and every other stripe in the upper wings. Also emboss the gold-painted eye-shaped areas. The body of the butterfly is gently embossed with the 3mm tool. Freehand emboss in the feelers of the

The finished card.

butterfly, using the pattern for guidance. With the stylus, draw a line down the centre of each of the large flower petals on the right side of the paper (this applies to five petals only – see the photograph for guidance), turn the paper over, and emboss the area between the central line and the outside edge of these petals until they are very white.

Emboss the gold-coloured petals and then, with the 3mm tool, the petals on either side of the gold-coloured ones to a pale grey colour. See the photograph for guidance. Emboss the leaves lightly with the 3mm tool and then, using the single-needle tool, draw a line down the centre of each leaf on the right side of the paper. Using the 1mm tool, emboss areas of central petal to give the chequerboard effect.

Finishing off

Fold the card and sew in any insert. Using either the single- or the two-needle tool, perforate round the scalloped edge of the card.

Optional: A hole can be pierced through the centre of each of the semi-circles that make up the border edge.

Using oil pastels in small areas

You can use oil pastels to colour small areas within a pattern, such as leaves or flower petals. To do this, apply the colour in the area you want but do not go right to the edge, as you will be able to spread the colour out to the edge. If you put too much colour on to the area you stand more chance of going over the edges of the designated area.

If you have a pointed end to your pastel, use this to apply the colour to the area. If you have pastels with two flat ends, take a piece of kitchen paper, fold it to a point, and use this to take colour off the pastel and apply to the parchment in the area you require. You can also take the colour off the pastel with your finger and apply to the area, but you will have to keep washing your hands. Some people have suggested that this can be done with a cotton bud but you will find that the cotton wool breaks up and the plastic stick then damages the parchment.

To spread colour in a designated area, simply fold the kitchen paper with the medium on so that you create a point and use this to spread the colour. Start in the middle of the area and then you can spread the pastel to the outer edges. This technique is used in the pattern on pages 51–53.

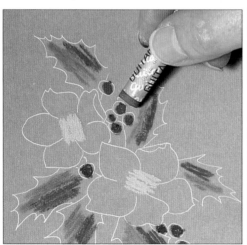

Applying colour with oil pastels.

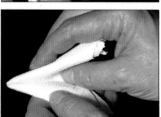

Folding kitchen paper to a point to spread oil pastels.

Spreading colour to the edge of the motif using folded kitchen paper and medium.

Christmas roses

*For a card with a different format, try turning
the motif on its side.*

Tracing

Mark the fold line with white pencil. With gold ink,
trace the greeting.

Trace the rest of the pattern with white ink, except
for the ends of the holly berries, which should be added
using black ink.

Oil pastel

Apply a little red or scarlet oil pastel to the middle of
each holly berry, this time working on the *right* side of
the paper.

Then turn the paper over and work from the back.
Using two different greens, place a stripe of one green in
one half of each holly leaf and a stripe of the other green
in the other half. Colour the central area of the flowers
with yellow oil pastel. Now spread the pastels in each
area, using a piece of kitchen paper folded to a point (as
shown on page 50).

When spreading the pastels in the holly leaves, use
the same method as for rainbow colouring and then
blend each green into the other in approximately the
middle of the leaf.

Embossing

With the 3mm tool, lightly emboss the holly berries. As
you applied the oil pastel to the *right* side of the paper,
the berries will remain pale red. With the 1.5mm tool
emboss the turned-over edge of the two flower petals.
With the 3mm tool lightly emboss the flower petals
from the *right side* of the paper. With the stylus tool,
make fine lines along the edges of the petals without a
turn-over, working on the *right side* of the paper and
working from the outside edge towards the centre.

Turn the paper over, and, working from the wrong
side, pierce holes in the area of the flower centre marked
on the pattern with a circle, using the single-needle tool.
Next, using the stylus, emboss the anthers round the
flower centres and then draw in the stamens using the
single-needle tool, working from anther to flower centre. On the *right side* of the paper use the stylus tool to
draw in the veins lightly in the holly leaves.

Emboss the greeting.

Finishing off

Fold the card and sew in any insert.

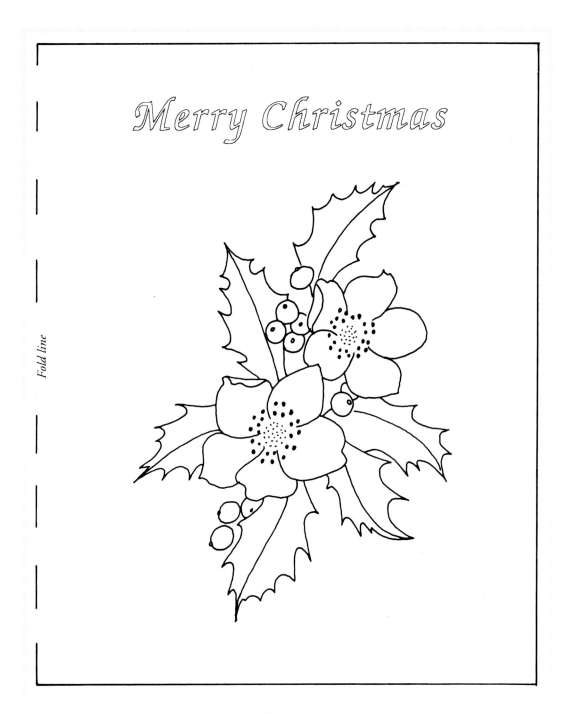

Merry Christmas

Fold line

Full-size pattern.

The finished card.

Using the parchment scissors

It takes a little practice to get used to the strange way in which the parchment scissors are held. Most people find it unhandy to start with but you do get the best results by holding them this way.

Hold the scissors in your left hand with the curved blades downwards. Insert the index finger into the first eye and the middle finger into the second eye. The scissors should rest in the first bend of the fingers and the thumb rests against the first eye of the scissors.

Do not open the blades of the scissors too wide, as this is not required for the work that they do. Try practising opening the scissor blades about 1mm (¹/₂₅in), which is the width between each four-hole perforation in lace work.

Insert the tip of the blades into the perforations (they should protrude about 1mm (¹/₂₅in) through the holes), turn the the blades slightly to the left, and cut. By turning the blades slightly you present a better cutting edge and also this forms the picot edge which is one of the hallmarks of the craft. I know that all this sounds very unhandy but it does work – and it does take practice! You really will obtain the best results this way.

The parchment scissors are used in this way when we wish to perforate out a piece of paper within a pattern. Perforate round the area with either the single-needle or the two-needle tool and then use the parchment scissors to cut the perforations. If we just pushed out these type of pieces then the paper would break and ruin all the hard work that went into the pattern. Some of the perforations in this type of work will simply break away naturally when we are using the scissors but there will be other places where this does not happen.

The next pattern will provide excellent practice in the use of the parchment scissors and will also help us when we go on to making the lace-like patterns so character-istic of and so much loved in this craft. We will be using the parchment scissors to remove perforated areas within the design.

See the next chapter for other ways of using the parchment scissors.

Flowers and trellis birthday card

You will need two sheets of A4 (11^3/$_4$ x 8^1/$_4$in) parchment paper: one for the front page with the cut-out area and one coloured, which will be the backing to the cut-out front page.

Tracing

Mark the fold line with white pencil and a ruler. With gold ink fill in the centres of the flowers and trace the greeting. Trace the remaining pattern with white ink. Do not trace the dotted lines within parts of the pattern as these indicate the areas to be perforated out.

Note: This pattern is reduced in size. To make it full size, simply enlarge it on a photocopier to 125 per cent of its present size.

Oil pastels

Using the second sheet of parchment paper, mark the fold line with white pencil and a ruler. We just need to colour half of the paper – that which appears behind the front page. Turn the paper over, and, using three colours of your choice, start in the top left-hand corner and put on bands of colour each at least 2.5cm (1in) wide.

I used my favourite three colours and started with a stripe of blue, then one of violet, then one of magenta. Carry on in this manner – blue, violet, magenta – until you finish off in the bottom right-hand corner. Then spread the colours and blend the area between the stripes so that one colour goes into the next. Finish off by wiping each area with clean dry kitchen paper.

Fold line

The finished card.

Embossing

Take the front page and turn it over. Now emboss the double lines between each flower and the double outer border as well as the double border round the greeting with the 3mm tool. With the 1mm ball tip, emboss the thicker lines of the greeting. With the 1.5mm tool, emboss the flower centres, and with the stylus tool or single-needle tool emboss tiny lines, working from the flower centre towards the outer end of each petal. See the photograph of the finished card for guidance.

Perforating

Using either the single-needle or the two-needle tool, perforate round the areas within each square. To give you an idea of what this means, some of the areas have been marked with dotted lines: these indicate the areas to be perforated. Repeat this with all the areas, so that we have a trellis-like pattern linked by flowers joining the greetings area to the outside border edge. Again, see the photograph of the finished card for guidance.

Cutting

Use the tiny curved parchment scissors to cut between the perforations you have made so that each area will fall out, leaving the trellis-like pattern.

Finishing off

Fold the outer card on the fold line, then fold the oil-pastel-coloured piece of parchment and sew this into the card with the coloured half backing the trellis pattern. Remember that the side you used the oil pastel on is the wrong side of the paper and this should be on the inside of the card. If you wish to put in a plain or coloured paper insert, then fold this and sew all three pieces together down the fold line. Trim the inserts level with the edges of the card.

Religious card

There may be times when you want to send a card with a Christian message. For those occasions, such as Easter, a christening, a First Communion, or a wedding, this card will be ideal. It would also be suitable as a condolence card. Add lettering to the card, or change your choice of oil pastel. For example, if you wish to use it as a sympathy card, use lilac or purple oil pastel on the reverse of the paper. For a wedding or christening, you can change the flower design.

Fold line

Full-size pattern.

The finished card.

Tracing

With white pencil, mark the fold line and the outer edges of the card. In silver, ink the outline of the double oval, the outline of the cross, and the circles within the cross shape. Trace the rest of the design in white ink.

Painting

Fill in the double oval with silver ink.

Oil pastel

On the front of the card, use two shades of green for the lily leaves and yellow for the stamens.

Embossing

With the single-needle tool and a ruler, draw in the cross-hatching in the cross. With the 1.5mm tool, emboss the double outline of the cross and the circles

within it. With the 3mm tool, emboss the oval around the cross, then gently emboss the leaves, working at an angle from the outside edge to the middle of the leaf on each side. Also, gently emboss the lower cup of the lily and the petal edges (see the photograph on page 58 for the effect required), then add a bit of extra embossing at the bottom of the cup where it joins the stem to give the effect of light catching it. With the 1.5mm tool, finish off the petal edges that you started with the 3mm tool so that they become very white. Emboss the central stamen, then emboss the turned-over edge on two of the lilies from the *front* of the paper. Now, with the fine point, draw in the central and side veins of the leaves on the *front* of the paper.

Perforating

With the single-needle tool, pierce a hole where each line intersects another in the cross. With the same tool, or the two-needle tool, perforate round the outline of the cross, taking care to leave four points of contact.

Cutting

Using the parchment scissors, cut through the perforations so that each quarter comes away.

Finishing off

Fold the card and sew in any insert with silver thread.

Using the four-needle tool to make lace

Most people want to start at this point and give little attention to the different forms of embossing which are the foundations of this very beautiful craft. The embossing of a lace grid gives the lace its character and in so many cases I have seen lace work that has given scant attention to the embossing or the correct use of the parchment scissors. This results in a piece that in no way resembles this ancient art.

You will need to have the patterns for this work photocopied, as you can only use the pattern a couple of times before it is destroyed by the pricking work. Photocopy from the original, not a photocopy, as each time a photocopy is copied it warps the pattern slightly, and open the book very flat to avoid any possible distortion of the image. Because of copyright laws, copies must be for your own use and not for onward sale.

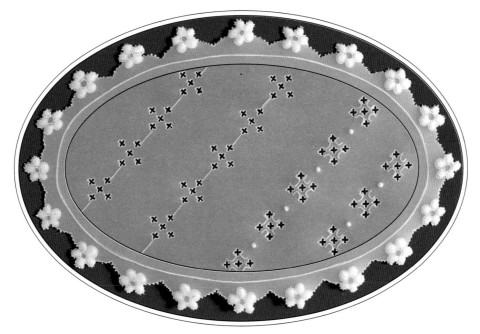

Making lace

1. Attach the parchment paper to the pattern and follow the tracing instructions. Then, using the felt pad and the four-needle tool, begin marking the grid.

Make sure that the four needles of the tool are square to the pattern to be marked or you will get a diamond shape amongst a row of squares. The needles should only travel half their length, as you are marking the grid in order that it can be embossed. If you let the needles travel the full length you could break the perforations when you emboss the design in the lace grid.

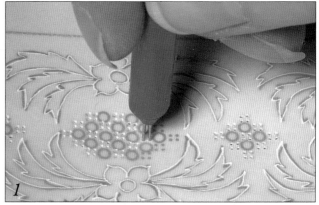

2. Once you have marked the four-needle grid, remove the parchment paper from the pattern, turn it over on to the embossing pad and emboss the design using the 1.5mm tool. Also emboss the design in the grid as shown by the pattern.

Never try to use oil pastels on a design that has been perforated: the effect is similar to using a nutmeg grater and it will spoil all your hard work. All oil-pastel work must be done before perforating; this sometimes means that you have to remove the pattern after tracing, use the oil pastels, and then attach the work back on to the pattern in order to mark the lace grids.

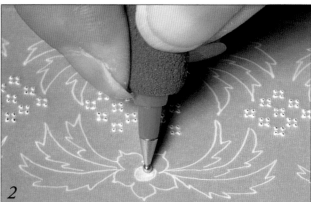

3. The tiny circles in a lace pattern mean that you should emboss the whole of the area between these perforations. Do not worry about squashing any of the perforations during embossing as you will be reperforating the design prior to cutting. Work from side to side in these areas and once the paper is elastic then you can go round and round. It will look square at the time of embossing, but once all cutting is complete it will take on a round appearance. The embossing should be very white as this gives the lace its character.

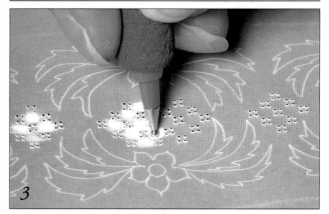

4. After you have completed all the embossing, turn the paper over to the right side and then, using the felt pad, reperforate the holes, allowing the needles to travel their full length. As most of the needle tools are not exactly square you will have to turn your tool until it matches the first holes, and after this you will be holding the tool in the same way as you did when you first marked the grid. By reperforating we have also made the holes the right size for the scissors.

1

2

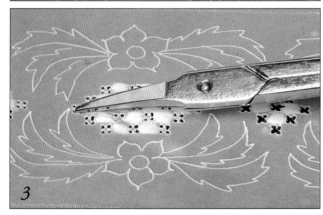

3

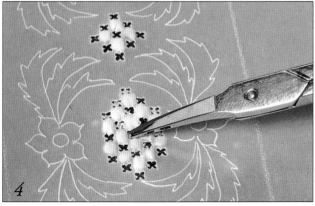

4

Cutting the perforations to crosses

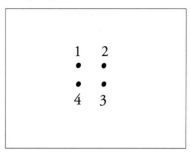

1   2
•   •
•   •
4   3

1. Turn the parchment so that the perforations are square to you and then insert the scissors into the holes numbered 1 and 2 on the diagram, turn the scissors slightly to the left, and cut. Cut all the top sets of holes that you have mentally numbered 1 and 2.

2. Turn the paper a quarter turn and cut holes 2 and 3, and once you have cut all the holes mentally numbered 2 and 3, turn the paper again a quarter turn.

3. Cut all the holes numbered 3 and 4.

4. Again give the paper a quarter turn and finally cut all the holes numbered 4 and 1.

I have tried to make this explanation as easy as possible. If you have cut correctly, you should have cross-like holes with embossing between them.

Now try this technique out on the pattern on page 62.

Tips on close-up work

For those of you who have eyesight problems I would suggest that you treat yourselves to a magnifying glass that either clamps to the table or will stand by itself on the table. If you are short-sighted you will probably not need this type of aid but you will need to sit in very good light, either by the window or under the light of a strong lamp.

Lacy bookmark

Tracing

Mark the outside edges of the bookmark with white pencil and a ruler. Trace the three leaves that protrude from each side of the flower in gold; trace the flowers themselves in white.

Perforating

Mark the four-needle grid.

Embossing

Emboss the pattern in the lace grid and the flower centres with the 1.5mm tool. Using the single-needle tool, draw in fine lines from the bottom of each flower petal, working towards the centre; also draw in veins on the leaves.

Cutting

Reperforate the four-needle grid and cut to crosses.

Finishing off

Cut round the outside edge of the bookmark and slip it into a ready-made bought bookmark sleeve.

Optional: When you have made this bookmark following the pattern above, you may wish to give it a different appearance when making it again. If so, using oil pastels *before* you mark the grid, colour the area where the larger lace grid goes with orange, the area of the leaves with green and the flower heads yellow, or any combination of colours that you wish. You can also perforate the long edges of the bookmark just outside the tracing line and then round or square off the ends with a pair of scissors.

Full-size pattern.

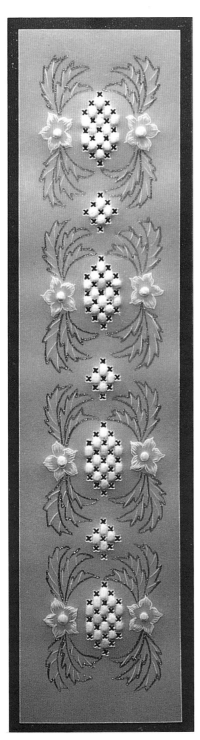

The finished bookmark – first version.

The finished bookmark – second version.

Carnival mask and orchid card

Tracing

Mark the fold line with white pencil. Trace the design with white ink, including the two double-outline borders.

Oil pastels

Colour the area between the outside border area and the middle oval border with dark blue oil pastel or a pastel the colour of your choice.

Perforating

Carefully put the card back on to the pattern and mark the four-needle grid area in the mask.

Embossing

With the 3mm tool, emboss both double borders and also the double outline of the mask edge and eye pieces, the mask stick and the bottom petal of the orchid. *From the right side of the paper,* emboss the other petals of the

Fold line

Full-size pattern.

The finished card.

orchid. *From the back of the paper,* using the 1.5mm tool, emboss the design in the lace grid and the alternate stripes in the mask stick, the two centre pieces of the orchid and the larger of the five petals in the corner flowers of the border, plus the centre of these flowers.

Emboss the circle at the bottom of the flower buds in the border, one half of each of the leaves in the border design, and alternate squares in the ribbon on the mask to give a chequerboard effect. With the single-needle tool, mark vein lines in the other half of the border leaves. With the stylus tool, emboss fine lines in the bottom two curves of the bottom petal of the orchid; also, *from the right side of the paper,* emboss fine lines at the tip of each of the rest of the orchid petals.

Cutting

Reperforate the lace grid and cut to crosses; then, using the single-needle tool, pierce a hole in the middle of each of the embossed areas in the lace grid.

Finishing off

Fold the card and sew in any insert. Perforate round the outer edge of the shaped border, working from the fold line round and back to the other end of the fold line.

Stylised butterfly

In this pattern we see that it is not always necessary to cut the four-needle grid: some of it can be left uncut to add to the decorative effect.

Tracing

Mark the fold line with white pencil and a ruler. Trace the scalloped border edge, the corner pieces and the outline of the butterfly's wings, body and antennae.

Perforating

Mark the four-needle grid in the wings and the inner-border diamond shapes.

Embossing

With the 3mm tool, emboss the double outline of the butterfly wings and the body pieces. With the 1.5mm tool, emboss the ends of the antennae and the double outline areas of the corner pieces. The two circles at the bottom of each corner piece are also embossed. With the stylus, draw round the outside edge of each diamond-shaped grid as shown on the pattern, emboss the four lines extending from each diamond, and also draw a line from corner hole to corner hole in the lace grid within the butterfly wings, which will produce a cross-hatched design.

Cutting

Reperforate the four-needle grids and cut the grid in the wings to crosses.

In the diamond grids, cut only the outside-edge perforations to crosses and also the middle four-hole perforation. You should leave the other sets of four-needle holes uncut.

Finishing off

Fold the card on the fold line and sew in any insert as required.

Variations

1. The area around the butterfly can be coloured with oil pastel to give a misty coloured background to the butterfly.

2. The whole of the area within the scalloped outline could be coloured with oil pastel of your choice.

Butterflies make lovely motifs to fill in with lace work.

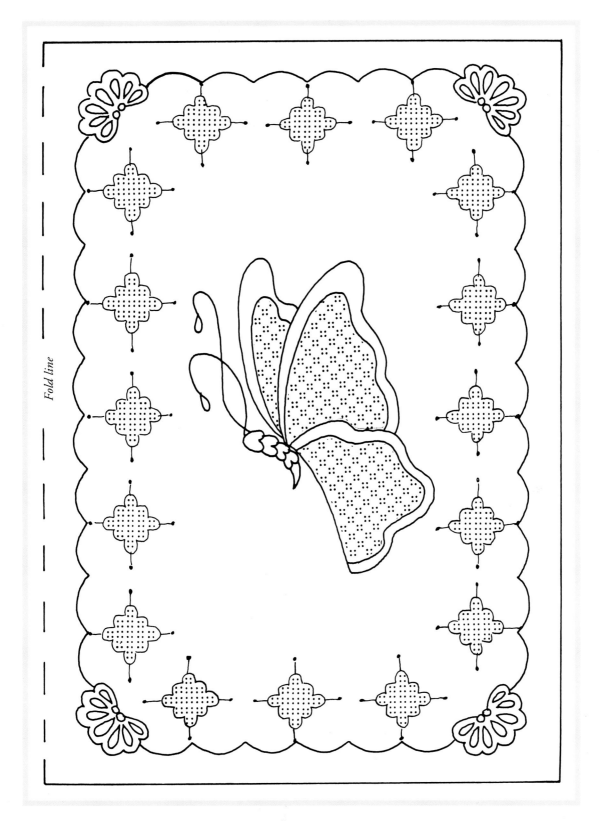

Fold line

Full-size pattern.

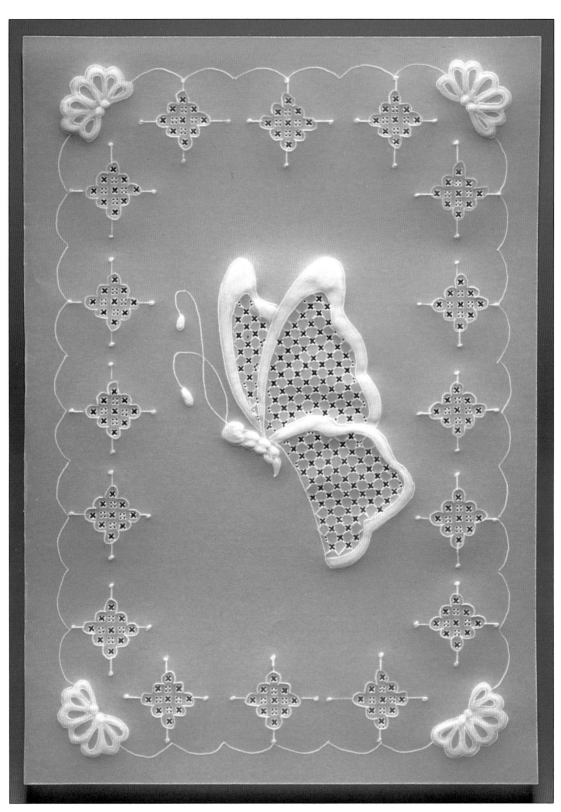

The finished card.

Cutting slots in lace work and freehand embossing

Cutting slots

Lace grids are composed of a series of four holes, as we have seen in the last three patterns, but if these holes are close together, instead of cutting to just crosses you can cut them to slots or corners.

A series of two to six four-hole grids shown close together usually denotes a slot to be cut. To do this, you prick and cut the four holes in the normal manner and then cut the dams between these crosses, using the same cutting technique. This forms a slot.

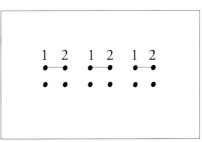

Cutting slots – diagram.

Freehand embossing

As you get more confident you will look at patterns and decide that you will freehand emboss in certain features – such as central motifs – without tracing them. It is often better if you emboss such things as flower petals shown in lace grids freehand rather than trace them and then emboss them. If you trace them I feel that you lose the delicacy of the design. It does not matter if you do not get all the petals even, as after cutting this will not be noticeable.

I usually try out a portion of such patterns on a spare piece of parchment so that I can get the placements right before I try it on the piece I am making.

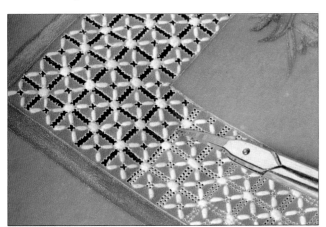

Cutting slots.

Chinese New Year card

I chose to design a card for the Chinese New Year as a way of saying thank you to my five sleeping partners – my Shih Tzu dogs. You can of course omit the ideograph, which reads Kung Hay Fat Choy (loosely translated as Happy New Year), and use either a monogram or a small design of your own choice.

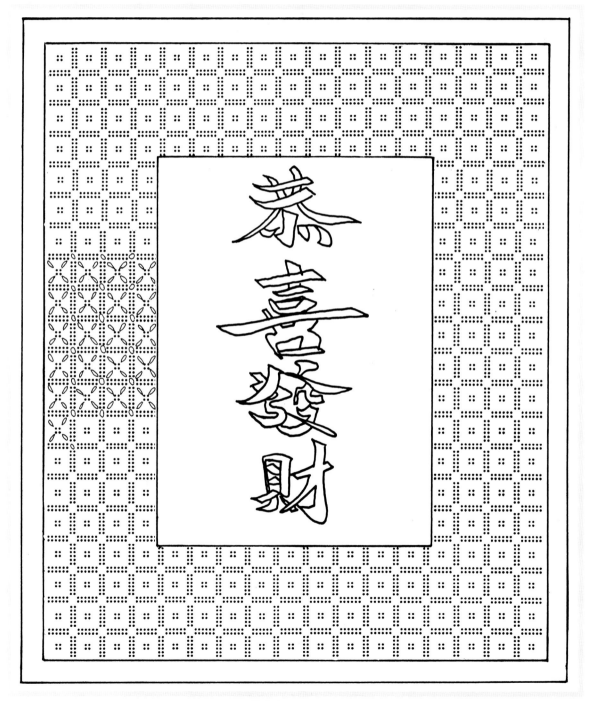

Full-size pattern.

Tracing

Ink the double outline, the inner border lines and the greeting in gold.

Painting

With gold ink, fill in the area between the double outline and the greeting outline.

The finished card.

Oil pastel

Colour the area of the perforation grid with red oil pastel.

Perforating

Mark the four-needle grid.

Embossing

Emboss the gold outer border, the greeting and the pattern in the lace grid.

Cutting

Reperforate the grid and cut to slots and crosses.

Finishing off

Fold the card and sew in the red insert with gold thread, then trim the edge of the card.

Oval lace card

Tracing

Mark the fold line and outer edges of the card with the white pencil. Trace the border round the oval and the oval line, the design within the circle, and the circle itself in white ink.

Oil pastels

Using a violet oil pastel, colour the area between the edge of the card and the oval. Using ochre, colour the area inside the circle.

Perforating

Mark the four-hole grid with the four-needle tool.

Embossing

With the 3mm tool, emboss all the scrolls round the oval and also the two leaves attached to each of the corner flowers. Also emboss the bell-like flower heads in the central design.

With the 1.5mm tool, emboss the centres of the four corner flowers and the top of the bell flowers where they join the stalk. Emboss the anthers and one half of the leaves in the central design. Emboss the design in the lace grid. With the stylus tool, draw in fine lines on the edges of the four corner flower petals, working from outside towards the centre, and also on the fluted bottom of each bell flower.

Emboss the rounded top of the bell flower, using the same fine lines but working from the rounded edge towards the centre. Draw in the veins on the leaves of the corner flowers.

Cutting

Reperforate the four-hole grid and cut the sets of two four-hole perforations to slots. Do not cut the four-hole perforation in the centre of each square: these are left uncut as part of the pattern.

Finishing off

Fold the card on the fold line and sew in any insert as required.

Fold line

Full-size pattern.

The finished card.

Exotic bird

This pattern includes slots in the lace border and also gives you your first opportunity of trying your hand at freehand embossing within a lace grid. The pattern also gives you practice for freehand embossing in the design itself. The long tail feathers amongst the more exotic ones should be feathered freehand; that is to say, trace the central portion of the feather as given on the pattern and then, using the single-needle tool, draw in the tiny lines on each side of the centre line.

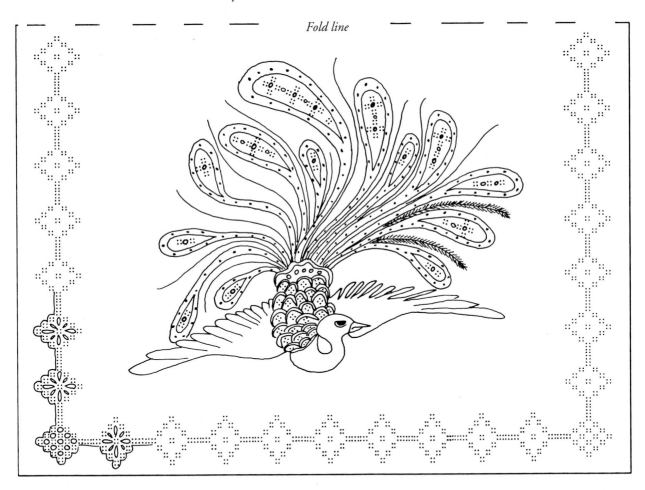

Fold line

Note: This pattern is reduced in size. To make it full size, simply enlarge it on a photocopier to 125 per cent of its present size.

Tracing

Mark the fold line with the white pencil. With white ink trace the rest of the design but *do not* trace the tiny dots in the borders of the large tail feathers or the feathering guide that appears on two of the tail feathers.

Oil pastels

Use magenta on the eye portions of the large tail feathers, dark blue in the area of the tail feathers shown as lines, and turquoise on the rest of the tail area.

The finished card.

Optional: you could use a colour of your choice for the body of the bird if you wished.

Perforating

Mark the four-needle grid in the border and also in the tail feathers and body feathers of the bird.

Embossing

Emboss the areas between the perforations on the large tail feathers as indicated by a small circle on the pattern; the double outline of the feathers on the bird's body; its beak and the black area of the eye; and the areas indicated in the two corner pieces of the border, using the 1.5mm tool. With the 1mm tool, freehand emboss tiny dots in the border area of the large tail feathers, using the pattern as guidance. Emboss the petals in the lace grid. With the plastic end of your tool, or the 3mm tool, lightly emboss the wings, neck and head of the bird.

Using the single-needle tool, freehand emboss in the feather lines on the flight feathers of the wings and on the line-like feathers in the tail. An example of two tail feathers has been shown on the pattern for guidance.

With the 1mm tool, emboss along the leading edge of the wings, starting at the body end and tapering out to nothing at the wing tips.

Also lightly emboss in tiny semi-circles on the main part of the wing and the neck of the bird to give the impression of the body feathers. With the stylus tool, draw a line round the outer edge of the lace border as shown on the pattern.

Perforating

Reperforate all the four-hole perforations. Cut the perforations in the large tail feathers to crosses and those in the border to crosses and slots. *Do not* cut the four-hole perforations on the bird's back.

With the single-needle tool, pierce holes between the embossed dots in the borders of the large feathers. Also pierce a hole through the centre of the embossed areas of the lace grid in these tail feathers, and in the five embossed circles of the bird's body where it meets the tail.

Finishing off

Fold the card on the fold line and sew in any insert.

Cutting out large corners in lace work

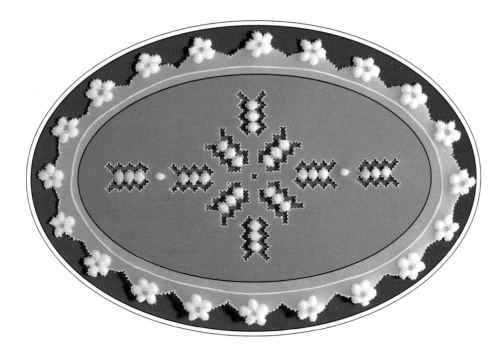

Sometimes a lace design calls for a whole piece to be perforated out to give a more open look: perhaps a corner, a diamond or a whole square.

On the pattern, the perforation grid will show the four holes close together as it does for a slot, but instead of being in a line it could just show a corner. You cut these perforations to crosses and then then cut the dams between the crosses just as you would when making slots, but in this case, instead of a strip of paper falling out you will get a whole corner or square.

In the next pattern there is again some freehand embossing in the lace grid: something a bit larger than you have tackled before. It does not matter if the embossed outlines are not all exactly the same – I cannot manage this either! The overall effect on the finished card will be fine.

Victorian fuchsias

Fold line

Note: This pattern is reduced in size. To make it full size, simply enlarge it on a photocopier to 125 per cent of its present size.

Tracing

Mark the fold line and outline of the card in white pencil. Trace the double border, the square and the circle, and the design within the circle, using white ink.

Oil pastels

Colour the area of the lace grid within the double border with orange, the area of the square (not the circle) with dark green and the circle with yellow. Choose any combination of three colours that you like; each colour scheme will give the card a different look.

Perforating

Mark the perforation grid.

Embossing

With the 3mm tool, emboss the area within the double outline and the flower-heads in the central design. Use the stylus tool to draw the bell-like flowers in the lace grid and the design around the single four-hole perforations. Also emboss in fine lines on the fluted edges of the central flowers, working from the bottom edge towards the centre and from the top edge where the

The finished card.

flower joins the stalk towards the centre. With the 1mm tool, emboss the anthers in the central design and also the the anthers of the flowers in the lace grid. Then, using the 1.5mm tool, fill in the outline of the flowers in the lace grid and emboss the leaves in the central design.

Cutting

Reperforate the lace grid and cut to crosses and corners.

Finishing off

Fold the card on the fold line and sew in the insert of your choice. Trim the card to size.

And finally...

Having worked your way through this book, you will now be able to tackle any sort of embossing or lace work with great confidence.

There are more techniques to be learnt in this craft, such as painting in inks or acrylics, and even three-dimensional work, but these are really the subject of another book! First you should practise and master all the basic skills you have learnt in this book.

Happy embossing!

Suppliers

Parchment-craft equipment and materials are widely available in craft shops under the name of *Pergamano*. If you have any difficulty in obtaining any of the items for this craft, please write to the Publishers for an up-to-date list of stockists, including mail-order suppliers.

Search Press Limited, Wellwood, North Farm Road, Tunbridge Wells, Kent TN2 3DR, England.

Index

ball-tip tools 30, 36
beeswax 11
birthday card 14, 18
bookmarks 28–29, 62–64
butterfly 44–46, 48–50, 66–68

Chinese New Year card 70–72
Christmas card 51–53
chrysanthemums 39–41
colouring 42–53
cross 57–59
cutting out large corners 77
cutting slots 69
cutting to crosses 61

daisies 14

embossing 8, 13–21, 69
envelopes 10
exotic bird 75–77

fan 22

flowers 26–27
four-needle tool 59
fuchsias 31–33, 78–80

gold ink 11

harebells 39–41
history 6

ink 10, 11–12
inserts 10, 16–17

mask 64–66
materials and equipment 8–10
medium 10, 43, 47

oil pastels 10, 42, 50
orchid 64–65

needle tools 8
numerals 18

pad 8
paintbrush 10
pansies 29–30
parchment paper 8
parchment scissors 10, 54–59, 61
pen 10, 11
pencil 10
perforating 22–23, 59–60

rainbow colouring 47
religious card 57–59
reversing the tool 28
ruler 10, 12

sewing 16–17
single-needle tool 22–23
stylus tool 36

tracing 11

Valentine card 34–35